A new view on the horizon

Zoe Seufert

BookLeaf Publishing

Presentation by *BookLeaf Publishing*

Web: www.bookleafpub.com

E-mail: info@bookleafpub.com

ISBN: 9789357212212

First edition 2023

I dedicate my poems to my lovely English teacher who has always inspired me to write more. I also dedicate this to my loving family who are the most supportive people I could wish for!

ACKNOWLEDGEMENT

For my family and friends, keep being your amazing selves.

PREFACE

Shoot for the moon, even if you miss you will land among the stars!
-Z.S

War

A war between wrong and right,
Those who choose not to listen but instead
choose to fight,
Always seen but never believed to be there,
Always heard but never bothered to care,
Always talked about but nothing ever done,
Always led by the powerful one,
World War II should have been the end not the
start,
Instead of creating one you choose to part,
Haven't you learned about those ancestors who
also started war
before,
Haven't you learned that you're making a bad
decision for all,
When will you start to listen and think,
When will you realise everyone should float not
sink,
Why don't you realise this all before,
Because in the end you will be left with nothing
at all,
Don't you see that your problem still isn't solved,
Haven't you seen all the people you have
involved,
Don't you get this isn't pretend,

Doesn't it bother you how many lives have come to an end,
To all those politicians out there,
You are killing small children, forced fathers, lost mothers,
Don't you care?

Disappointment

Imagine someone believes in you,

And expects a one but you deliver a two,

Imagine if you are meant to understand,

But when you are meant to answer you miss the command,

If everyone looks up to you,

But all you can give is the wrong review,

When the looks of sympathy pass,

And the chatter starts up in the class,

Imagine everyone doing better than you,

Imagine the feeling of being looked through,

When you don't pass a test,

And you become depressed,

Imagine the disappointment coming from within,

They don't even know where to begin,

Imagine them wishing that others where like you,

Imagine feeling the feeling of blue,

When you fail over and over again,

Imagine they start feeling the disappointment then,

When you are all alone,

And you are in the "good try" zone,

Imagine them never believing in you ever again,

Imagine the feeling of never being considered, instead given the job of holding the pen,

Imagine being the disappointment in someone's life,

Imagine never being as strong as a knife,

Imagine a lonely grey world right next to the successful one,

Imagine everyone thinking that you're dumm,

Imagine missing someone's most important appointment

Just imagine being a disappointment…

The feeling of getting lost in a book

It all started when I read my first book,

I was captured with just one look,

As I turned the pages,

I realised that there are many books for my ages,

But I had to finish the book to be pleased,

I read through the pieces of paper at lightning speed,

I inhaled the information with greed,

I must know the end, so I read, and I read,

It is pulling me deeper dragging me on a lead,

The world outside starts to fade,

As I continue to turn the page,

Soon the world I live on is gone,

And I could have sworn,

That I was put into a new universe,

I can see this isn't a curse,

When I realise that I am the main character,

I have broken some sort of barrier,

That has engulfed me hole,

My creativity is out of control,

A massive monster is heading this way,

I know that I must save the day,

I grab a sword that is on the wall,

As I stand up tall,

I charge at the beast,

Who is having quite a feast,

And stab it in the toe,

He howls in pain making quite a show,

Before he starts thrashing his arms at me,

He misses and knocks over the tea,

From then on it is a battle,

With lots of clitters, clatters and rattles,

I look around and form a plan,

I am going to make a ban,

So that no one will ever forget me,

I will let everyone live free,

I run up the hill,

Standing still,

I shout at the monster to look,

The monster doesn't look shook,

So, when it turns, I stab it in the heart,

But that is just the start,

As it falls, I tie it up in rope when something washes over me,

As a feeling is growing inside of me,

The monster seems sad,

I feel bad,

I think I understand,

The monster is simply different like you and me,

Just like how an otter is different to a bee,

It is just lonely,

It feels like it is the only,

One who doesn't have a friend,

I know this can't be the end,

So, I hatch my idea to the crowd,

Who are starting to grow loud,

Giving ideas for me to use,

I now must choose,

How to tell the creature,

Who has some lovely features,

As I tell it my idea,

It doesn’t seem to be in fear,

Of ever being lonely again,

It will work in the library of Ken Chen,

As a comforter to children so that they can learn how to read,

I stare at them from outside with plead,

But I am frozen in time,

This book of mine,

Has no more pages for me to explore,

When I really want more,

I come back to the real world,

I am still curled,

In my beanbag safe and sound,

I see something on the ground,

Another book for me to read,

But for now, I must go to sleep.

Questions

How do you define something that isn't there,

How do you tell the difference between wrong
and unfair,

Is the opposite of the opposite the opposite or
the same,

When two people do something wrong who is to
blame,

Which way do the stairs go,

What is the difference between a performance
and a show,

Why does the fridge have a light, but the freezer
does not,

Why doesn't our school have a team mascot,

Why are boys and girls not seen as equal,

What is the difference between google translate
and DeepL,

If you are waiting for the waiter does that make you the waiter or the waiter the waiter,

If two people come late who is later,

Are oranges named after the colour or is the colour named after the fruit,

How does a teacher know when you are talking if you are on mute?

Body Image

Make-up plastered on their face,

Not a single hair can be out of place,

Afraid of their own reflection,

Wanting to be the impossibly perfection,

Obsessed with their weight,

Having a single, little raison on their dinner plate,

Exercising nonstop,

Never eating about to drop,

Just to be thin or beautiful,

In cloths barely movable,

Always worried about what others think,

Always needing to be in perfect sync,

Obsessed with being the most popular,

Always needing to be friends with the most spectacular,

You can never go wrong with just being you,

One day you will see it too.

Fire

It spreads around the innocent scene,

Think of everything before being healthy and
green,

After it comes everything turns black,

Eating up everything on its track,

It is greedy and vicious,

Golloping up the important food very nutritious,

Leaving behind skeletons in its wake,

Nothing standing all just bending it leaves the
trees in ache,

It only grows stronger the more it must eat,

It builds up more and more strength as it doubles
the heat,

Bigger and bigger it grows,

But at the end of the forest it froze,

Nothing left to see,

Only it can’t just let it be,

It rages on and on,

The city stands tall as white as a swan,

The blue and red lights paint the sky above,

They shoot out water with great care and love,

The water hugs the fire with a long cooling hug,

The fire is calming down into a shrug,

Only gently calmed into a small cast,

Peacefully asleep at last.

What people want

Most people dream to become famous,

Some wish to live a life painless,

Others want to be filthy rich,

Some want to always give the perfect pitch,

The majority of people want to find unbreakable love,

Others want the newest most expensive baseball glove,

Some want to become president,

Others want people to pay their rent,

Many wish to have magical powers,

Most people want a palace of flowers,

Many want to look like a perfect barbie,

Some want to throw an endless party,

All people want are impossible things,

Wanting people to propose with diamond rings,

Some want life to never feel crappy,

But none of that matters if you are not happy.

Leaf

Red, orange, yellow and green,

The prettiest thing I have ever seen,

Slowly parachuting down in the autumn breeze,

Patching up the ground with ease,

Leaves in all shapes and sizes,

A miracle not worthy of prices,

As unique as a snowflake,

As delicate as a cake,

Worth all the time and money just to see,

Mother Nature decorating for the season to be.

Advent calendar

The morning excitement,

Every day a new requirement,

Opening your little secret door each day,

Enjoying your secret sweet on your way,

Each day leads closer to Christmas,

Making letters to Santa for his forgiveness,

Day one, two, three, four, five, six

Nikolaus bringing a load of fun and tricks,

The fun of opening a little present before the big day,

With many shades of red, green, white and grey,

Day seven, eight, nine, ten, eleven and twelve,

Watch out for your elf on the shelf,

The naughty little fellow hiding around your house,

Quietly running around the house sneaking around like a mouse,

Day thirteen, fourteen, fifteen, sixteen, seventeen, eighteen,

Everyone getting the house clean,

Families decorating the Christmas tree,

Houses with the Christmas spirit live a few days worry free,

Ornaments hang high for all to see,

Day nineteen, twenty, twenty-one, two, three,

What a lovely day to be,

One more day before endless presents,

Listening to a bunch of Christmas segments,

Day twenty-four,

The final door,

Christmas is upon us at last,

It is time for a blast,

Carols at night,

Full of glee not fright,

A massive feast,

Presents as big as a beast,

Chatter for hours on an end,

Using your toys to help you pretend,

You wake up on Christmas day,

Another day to celebrate,

A round of friends and family,

Around people singing casually,

Another round of unique gifts,

As the mood of everyone lifts,

Day twenty-six

Left over cake mix,

A massive mess oh dear,

We will all have to wait for Christmas to come next year.

The Vessel

No matter how big or strong,

A power that can change you whole,

An ability so bright,

It's hard to describe,

The power to change fright,

And turn it into the power of right,

Where everything you choose is chosen,

A king, a queen or a burden,

All you do is close your eyes,

Block out the world and prepare a sight,

A world of your creation just open the door,

And see what it has in store,

The world you imagine big or small,

Will give you the power to imagine more,

Just let yourself be free,

The greatest vessel you will see,

With the strength to carry an elephant and a bee,

Just remember you are free,

Your imagination can carry far and wide,

Just feel free and don't hide!

Covid Test

At the table I wait,

As the timer ticks down to eight,

The lines appear,

I have a fear,

That I am positive again,

I stutter and stumble,

I clatter and grapple,

With the answers in my hand,

My eyes are peeled,

Will my fate be sealed,

By the virus again,

I focus hard,

I look at the card,

That shows me the start

Of the answer that lies ahead,

Many are selected

By the public again

As I look,

I feel shook

And inspect my future below,

To my surprise positive aren't I,

I am negative again!

Duckling

The little yellow duckling all lonely by the bay,

She watches the other ducklings have fun while they play,

The little yellow duckling sleeps alone in the grass,

She watches the other ducklings walking past,

The little yellow duckling swims alone in the water,

Her mother doesn't even notice her own daughter,

The little yellow duckling eats a tiny little fish,

She watches as the others share a grand fish dish,

The little yellow duckling sees a lonely gosling in the bush,

She decides to help the gosling by playing a game of push,

Gosling and Duckling have become friends,

They will be together until their life comes to an end,

Gosling and Duckling share missed happy times,

They write many poems of their friendship going on for many lines,

Gosling and Duckling have a blast,

Happy together at last.

Post Office

A big red box full of mysteries,

Full of someone's written histories,

A pile of letters and cards,

Travels away many yards,

To people who are far away,

Delivering your messages on their way,

Whether rain or sun,

The moment you see it is very fun,

Fancy letter arriving at your door,

The more you'll want more,

Many people scattered around the globe,

The number of letters could fill a wardrobe,

But they serve with pride,

One step then a long stride,

Bringing letters in the holidays,

They run around in an endless maze,

The only way they sleep at night,

Is when they have accomplished their letter fight.

Different

You shine so bright when you want to blend in,

When you want to lose you have to win,

You look so different, and people stare,

When you need to go you don't know where,

You make mistakes accidentally,

Others act with words, but you act physically,

The problem with modern society,

They forget we come with a wide range of
variety,

We forget none of us are the same,

When you feel emotions, you shoot out a flame,

A friend in life that is like you,

Can be all you need to push through,

In your darkest moments something positive will emerge,

A unique friendship will merge,

Your life will look better,

You can ignore the hate letter,

The stares become invisible,

Your sad life won't be miss able,

Life will be better with you and your friend,

Even if your friend is just pretend.

Friends

Thank you to you who makes me smile,

You make my life worth the while,

I am glad you are here,

You make my life's purpose clear,

You cheer me up when I am down,

You make me feel like negativity isn't around,

You're always there for me,

When I am with you, I am free,

Many boulders may lie ahead,

But true friends are like an unbreakable thread,

I will always be there for you,

I will help you when you feel blue,

And if your happiness starts to fade,

And your hair changes shade,

I will change my hair, my house and my style,

Just to see you for a longer while,

And when you pass away,

I will lay flowers by your grave every day,

Because even if I can't speak with you anymore,

Having spent my life with you is a score.

Stars

During the day,

They hide away,

In the night,

They come alive,

Whether rain or clear skies,

It illuminates the night air with its unique shines,

Make a wish to live up to one day,

Blow it up to the stars gently and watch it fly away,

Each day you can look up at the stars,

They will except you no matter how many scars,

All are equal, all is fair,

They have the time for happiness to share,

A dream could become reality,

An ocean on a rough sea,

Help your dream make others happy,

Enjoy a world less crappy.

Teachers

They advance our minds,

They play with our thoughts,

They set out our achievements,

And work on our faults,

They inspire a heart,

With the rough and the sooth,

They can help light our path,

And they guide the youth,

For our future now less frightened,

With each lesson you teach,

Each working hour you lengthened,

Each goal you help reach,

For each dusk of a genius,

Each mathematician and king,

It all started with a teacher,

And the knowledge they bring.

Halloween

We are in the spooky season,

So, listen closely for a good reason,

As the line between the dead and our normal life thin,

We must be certain we don't let them haunt us and win,

The pumpkins will glow,

The ghosts will show,

The witches will cackle,

The hunters known as the jackal,

Will howl the night away,

The dead plants will sway,

The spiders will play,

The evil will rise,

The ones we despise,

Will follow us all the way,

All the children will be most vulnerable,

As they are easily sufferable,

Their costumes can't trick the real,

They can easily steal,

Yet still no one believes,

They will watch from the trees,

As one by one the children collect their last bits of candy!

Dreamcatcher

Catch my nightmares make them go,

Illuminate my dreams with your glow,

Make me happy make me proud,

Chase away my angry cloud,

Keep me in Dreamland where nothing is bad,

Keep me occupied with fun stuff and lock away the sad,

Fulfill what I can't in the waking world,

Let me bounce, swing, jump, play and sleep comfortably curled,

Let my dreams never come to an end,

Help me forget that this is only pretend,

Because when my dreaming time is done,

I will wake up to a real sun,

Everything I learned today,

Will get me through another day.

Save our environment

If you see litter on the streets,

Or are overwhelmed by all the pollution,

If you feel like everything is something which repeats,

Remember there is always a solution,

There is always something we can all do,

To keep our water sources clean,

Keep the water flowing blue,

And keep our planet green,

Help by cleaning up your rubbish,

And recycle bottles and cans,

Reuse your old luggage,

And help others understand,

Single use plastic,

Lasts longer than you and me together,

It may not seem dramatic,

But it’s definitely not clever,

It doesn’t have to be a lot,

We should each do our share,

Just clean up a spot,

And show the environment you care,

The Earth needs you,

To adjust your way,

Save bamboo,

Help day by day,

Small changes are easy,

Just try it and you will see,

Help the air be a little more breezy,

By listening to me,

If we all use less,

The better the world would be,

It will relieve animals stress,

And make a difference you will see.

Music

All of the orchestras you see,

Are full of instruments from many different lands,

Making them not seem like a community,

But played together it is purely hearts and hands,

They practice for hours and days,

Each musician making a choice,

Each master plays and plays,

Giving their instrument a voice,

Guitars and Ukuleles make a lovely song,

Violins and Cellos beautiful as can be,

One by one they know they belong,

All together in the string family,

Flutes and oboes make a gorgeous tune,

Picolos and clarinets together are a fantasy,

Hearing them make flowers bloom,

All together in the woodwind family,

Cymbals and Gongs are really loud,

Drums and Timpanis shouldn't be taken casually,

They attract quite a crowd,

All together in the percussion family,

Trumpets and horns can make quite a show,

Trombones and tubas always sounding happily,

They can play high, medium and low,

All together in the brass family,

Pianos and keyboards are soft and bold,

Organs and electric keyboards are played amazingly,

Mythical to all those told,

All together in the keyboard family,

Some people aren't recognised for their brilliance,

Our amazing conductor keeps everyone on key,

They do have a lot of resilience,

Together forever in the music family!

www.ingramcontent.com/pod-product-compliance
Lightning Source LLC
Chambersburg PA
CBHW051736130826
49812CB00033B/891
9789357212212